COMPOSTING
Nature's Recyclers

by Robin Koontz
illustrated by Matthew Harrad

PICTURE WINDOW BOOKS
Minneapolis, Minnesota

Thanks to our advisers for their expertise, research, and advice:

Jeffrey R. Pribyl, Ph.D.
Professor of Chemistry and Geology
Minnesota State University, Mankato

Susan Kesselring, M.A., Literacy Educator
Rosemount–Apple Valley–Eagan (Minnesota) School District

_____

Editors: Jacqueline Wolfe and Nick Healy
Designers: Ben White and Brandie E. Shoemaker
Page Production: Joseph Anderson
Creative Director: Keith Griffin
Editorial Director: Carol Jones
The illustrations in this book were created digitally.

This book was produced for Picture Window Books by
Bender Richardson White, U.K.

Picture Window Books
1710 Roe Crest Drive
North Mankato, MN 56003
www.capstonepub.com

Library of Congress Cataloging-in-Publication Data
Koontz, Robin Michal.
Composting : nature's recyclers / by Robin Koontz;
illustrated by Matthew Harrad.
p. cm.
Includes bibliographical references (p.).
ISBN-13: 978-1-4048-2194-1 (hardcover)
ISBN-10: 1-4048-2194-5 (hardcover)
ISBN-13: 978-1-4048-2200-9 (paperback)
ISBN-10: 1-4048-2200-3 (paperback)
1. Compost—Juvenile literature. I. Harrad, Matthew, ill.
II. Title.
S661.K66 2007
631.8'75—dc22   2006008316

Table of Contents

Steaming Heap

It is a cool morning. A huge heap stands in the corner of a yard. It looks like a pile of leaves and sticks. Steam rises from the heap.

Put your ear next to the heap, and you might hear rustling. Look closely, and you might see things moving. Sniff the heap, and you might smell something. What is this steaming, rustling, moving, smelly heap? It is a compost pile.

FUN FACT

Some birds lay their eggs in piles of leaves and sticks. The heat of the pile helps to keep the eggs warm.

5

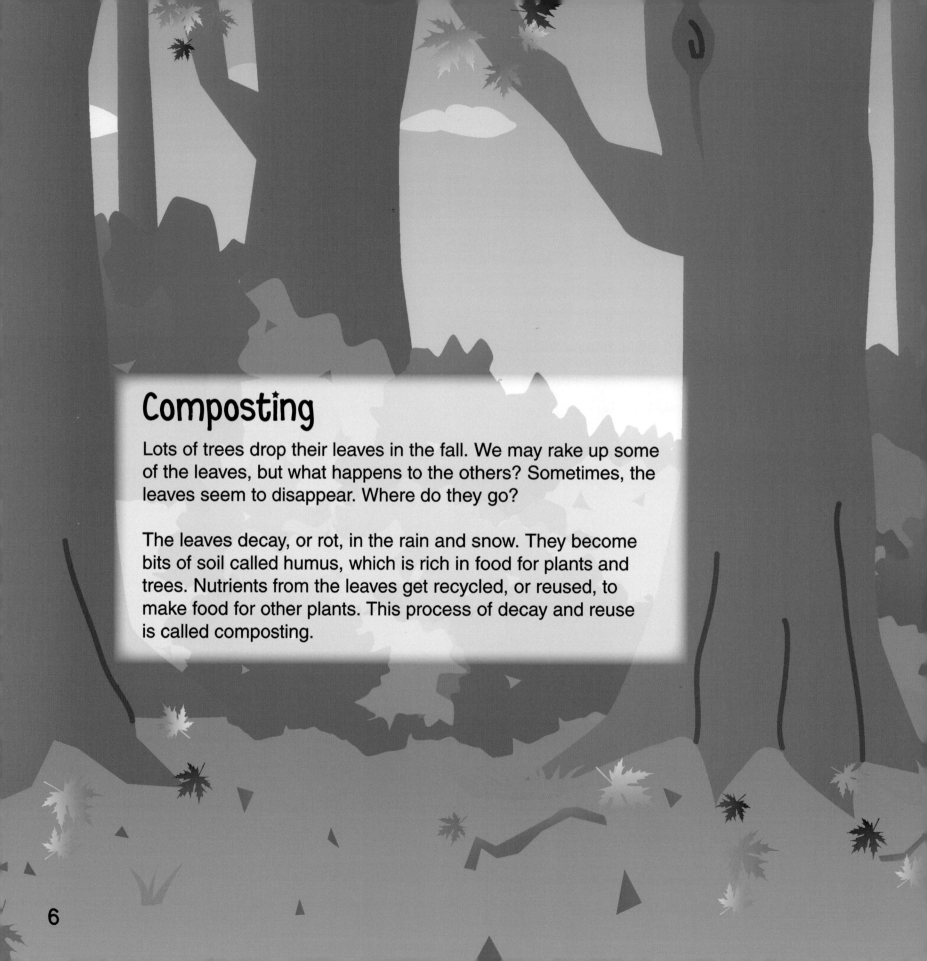

Composting

Lots of trees drop their leaves in the fall. We may rake up some of the leaves, but what happens to the others? Sometimes, the leaves seem to disappear. Where do they go?

The leaves decay, or rot, in the rain and snow. They become bits of soil called humus, which is rich in food for plants and trees. Nutrients from the leaves get recycled, or reused, to make food for other plants. This process of decay and reuse is called composting.

FUN FACT

The bigleaf maple has huge leaves—sometimes
as large as 18 inches (45 centimeters) across.

Homemade Food

One day, a tree will fall. Insects will eat the tree, and woodpeckers will peck holes in the bark to eat the insects. Other animals will find the woodpecker holes and move in. The tree will become a source of food and a home for many animals.

In time, all parts of the tree will decay. With a lot of help, the parts will compost and become humus. The humus will help new plants grow where the tree once stood.

FUN FACT

Scientists think the oldest tree in the world is a bristlecone pine tree in California. It is more than 4,750 years old. A sample, called a core, taken from the tree tells the tree's age by showing the number of tree rings.

Doing What Nature Does

Plants need sunlight, warmth, water, and air to grow. Plants also need humus, which is made from composting. In nature, plants and trees make humus by recycling their garbage. Can we recycle our garbage to make humus?

Yes, we can. We can make a compost heap, and we can feed our plants with it. Many things can be used for composting. We can recycle all kinds of garbage!

FUN FACT

In early times, farmers put a dead fish in the soil next to the seed they were planting. These farmers weren't trying to grow a fish! The fish decomposed, or rotted, and became humus. The humus helped the seed grow.

11

Heap Needs

A compost heap needs green or other colored things that are fresh, such as cut grass, orange peels, and egg shells. The heap also needs brown things that are dry, such as fallen leaves, sticks, and pine needles. Everything should be organic, or made from living things.

A compost heap also needs to stay damp. Give it some air, too. It won't take long before the heap gets busy!

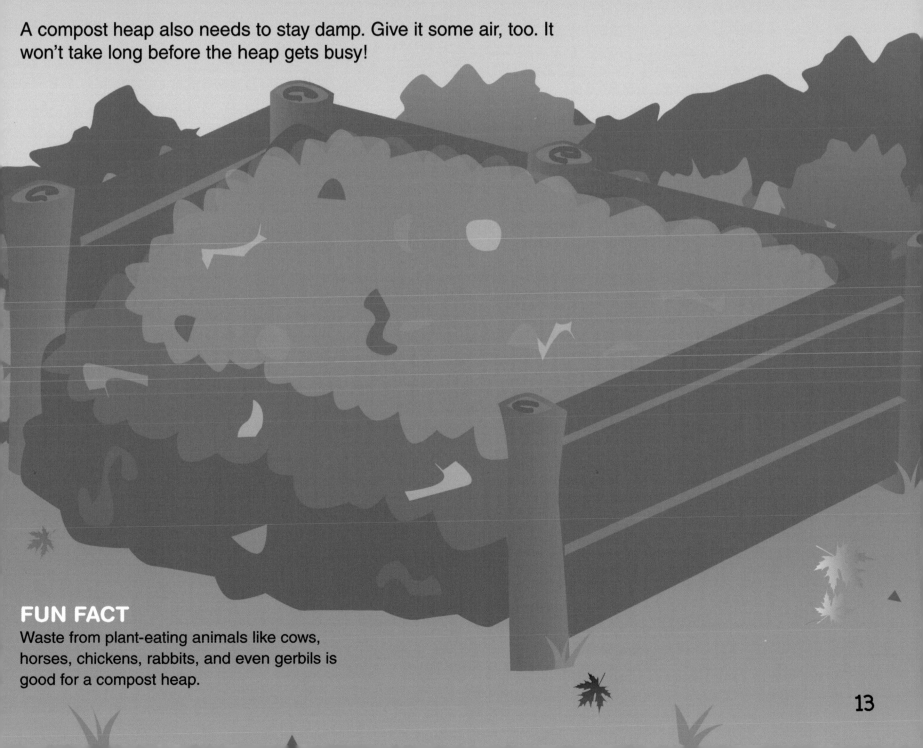

FUN FACT

Waste from plant-eating animals like cows, horses, chickens, rabbits, and even gerbils is good for a compost heap.

The Decomposers

All that green and brown stuff is yummy to lots of animals! Flies and beetles will be the first to come. They lay eggs that hatch into grubs that munch on the heap. Slugs and snails love to help, too.

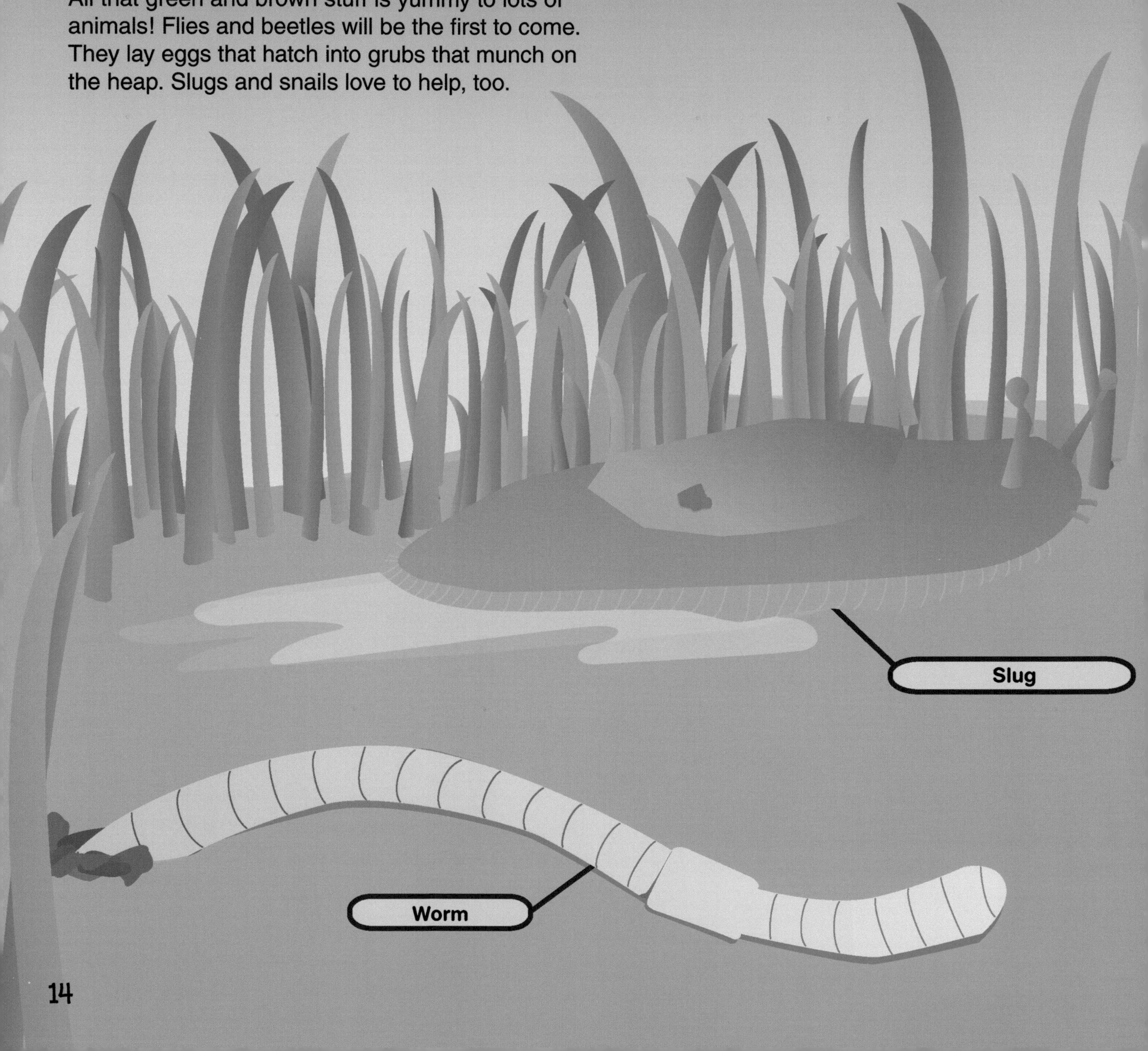

Slug

Worm

Soon the heap is full of decomposers. These are organisms that help leaves and trees to decay. Decomposers cut and chew their way through the compost heap. They leave behind their waste as they go. Their work turns the big pieces of compost into smaller pieces.

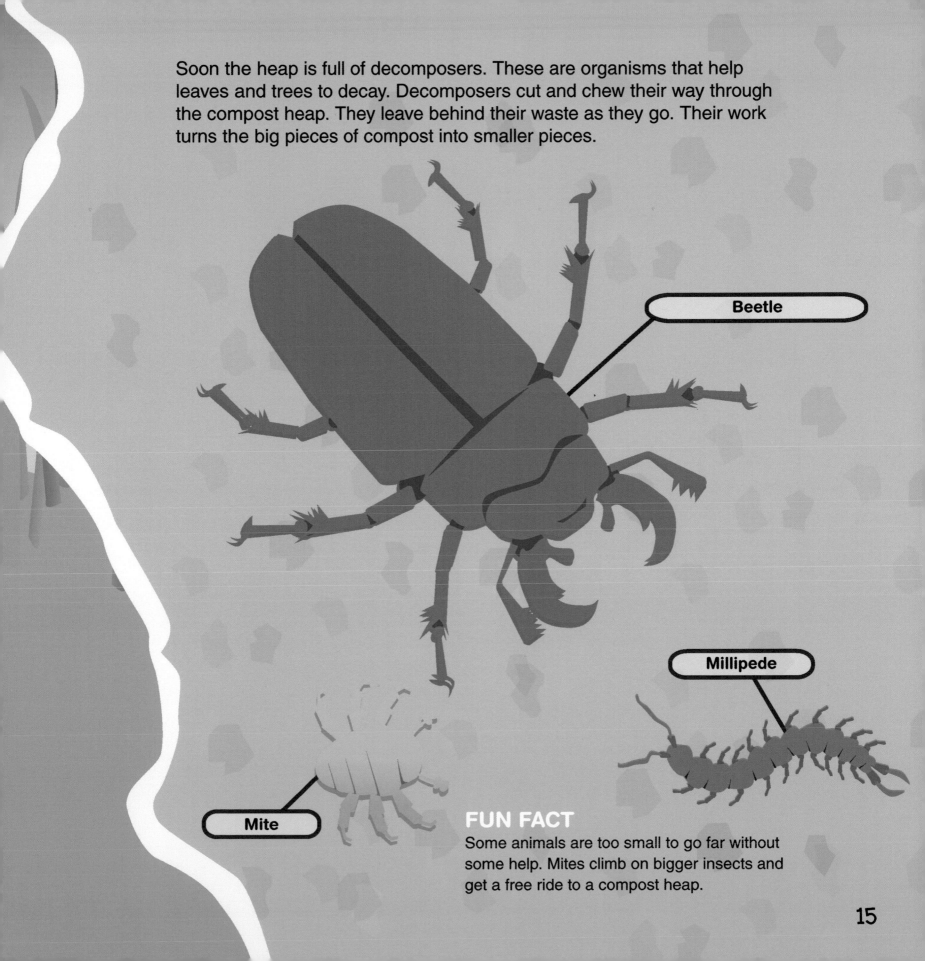

Beetle

Millipede

Mite

FUN FACT

Some animals are too small to go far without some help. Mites climb on bigger insects and get a free ride to a compost heap.

Lots of Food for Everyone

Spiders stalk other bugs on the heap. Ants, earwigs, and woodlice crawl all over. Worms wiggle inside. Most of the animals eat the garbage, but many of them also gobble up each other!

Decomposers heat up the heap. The heat helps the heap decompose even faster. You might see steam come from the heap on a cool morning. You might also smell an odor— the smell of decomposition at work.

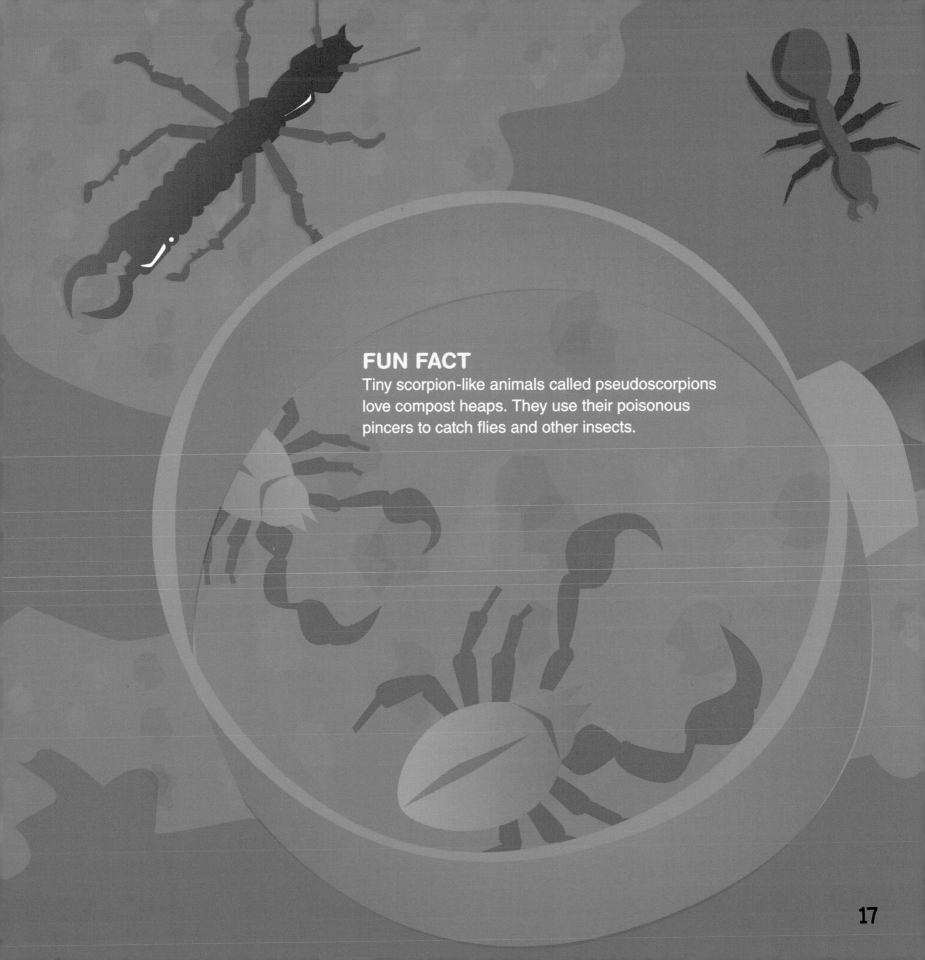

FUN FACT

Tiny scorpion-like animals called pseudoscorpions love compost heaps. They use their poisonous pincers to catch flies and other insects.

Mini-Munchers

The smallest decomposers in the heap are fungi and bacteria. Fungi come in many shapes and forms, such as molds and mushrooms. Bacteria are so tiny that we can't see them without a microscope. Even though we can't watch them do it, these little decomposers work the hardest of all.

Different kinds of fungi and bacteria have been eating the heap all along. But thanks to the bigger decomposers, now the little ones can finish the job.

Under the Microscope: Fungi

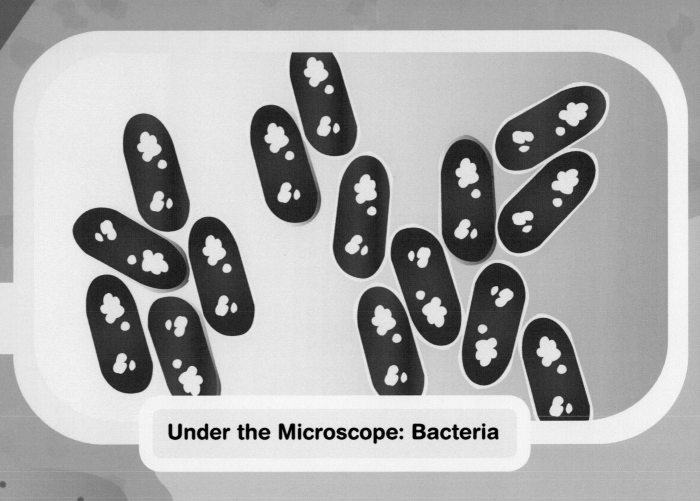

Under the Microscope: Bacteria

FUN FACT

Thousands of miles of fungi threads can spiral through a compost heap. There can also be 10 million bacteria in a spoonful of compost.

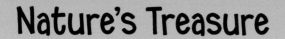

Nature's Treasure

When the heap is finished, it is much smaller. All of the decomposers worked hard. They turned the compost heap into a pile of humus, crawling with worms.

The composted humus is now ready to use—worms and all. Put the humus around your plants and trees, and watch them grow. What used to be trash is now treasure!

FUN FACT

Almost 60 percent of garbage in the United States, including paper, is material that could be composted. An average-size family's yard waste can help make about 300 pounds (136 kilograms) of compost a year.

21

Compost in a Bag

What you need:
- a medium-size heavy-duty plastic bag
- a twist tie
- garden and kitchen waste and some dirt

What you do:
1. Put 1/2 cup (1/8 liter) of shredded green or colored stuff such as tea leaves, coffee grounds, fruit peels, and grass clippings in the bag.

2. Add 1/2 cup (1/8 L) of shredded brown stuff such as pine needles or dry leaves.

3. Add 1 cup (1/4 L) of dirt. You need dirt because it will contain the tiny decomposers that will do the composting work.

4. Add 1 tablespoon (15 milliliters) of alfalfa pellets (rabbit food) and 1 ounce (30 mL) of water.

5. Seal the bag, and shake it well.

6. Squeeze the bag once a day to mix things up. Every other day, leave the bag open.

7. If all goes well, you will have composted humus in about 6 weeks! You can use it for your houseplants or outside plants.

What other kitchen waste could you add to your compost heap?

Why do you think you need to open the bag every other day?

Do you think composting will work faster in summer or winter? Why?

Compost Extras

Wasted Food

Americans throw away about 10 percent of the food they buy at the supermarket. That is more than 21 million shopping bags full of food being dumped every year. You can save kitchen waste in a plastic bag or can. Use it in your compost heap.

Let the Worms Do the Work

If you don't have room for a big heap, you can build a small worm bin and use up the kitchen garbage. Go to the library for a book on "worm bins" or "vermicomposting." One pound (0.45 kilograms) of worms can chew up one-half of a pound (0.23 kg) of food waste every day.

Solving a Smell

If your heap stinks, it probably needs more air. Turn it so the insides are on the outside. Add sawdust if possible. Also, if you build your compost heap on a pile of sticks, it will get more air.

Glossary

bacteria—simple, tiny forms of life that are decomposers, among other things
compost—to mix organic materials together; also the name given to the mixture of organic materials
decompose—to rot or break down
decomposers—creatures that break down organic materials and eat them
fungi—forms of life that include mushrooms, molds, and mildews; they live by decomposing organic material
humus—the finished product from composting
microscope—a tool that makes objects appear larger
organic—part of an animal or plant
organisms—living beings
stalk—to hunt

To Learn More

At the Library

Bailey, Jill. *Life in a Garbage Dump.*
Chicago: Raintree, 2004.
Pfeffer, Wendy. *Wiggling Worms at Work.*
New York: HarperCollins, 2004.
Ross, Michael. *Re-Cycles.* Brookfield,
Conn.: Millbrook Press, 2002.
Tomecek, Steve. *Dirt.* Washington, D.C.:
National Geographic Society, 2002.

On the Web

FactHound offers a safe, fun way to find Internet sites related to this book. All of the sites on FactHound have been researched by our staff.

1. Visit *www.facthound.com*
2. Type in this special code for age-appropriate sites: 1404821945
3. Click on the FETCH IT button.

Your trusty FactHound will fetch the best sites for you!

Index

Look for other books in the Amazing Science series:

Erosion: Changing Earth's Surface
   1-4048-2195-3
Magnification: A Closer Look
   1-4048-2196-1
Science Measurements:
   How Heavy? How Long? How Hot?
   1-4048-2197-X
Science Safety: Being Careful
   1-4048-2198-8
Science Tools:
   Using Machines and Instruments
   1-4048-2199-6